Teams Win
Teams Work

Copyright © 2005 by Ron Kaufman
All rights reserved. The moral right of the author has been asserted.

Published by Ron Kaufman Pte Ltd. - 10 9 8 7 6 5 4 3 2 1

Lift Me Up! - Teams Win, Teams Work!
ISBN 981-05-2934-1 - **136 pages.**

1. Teamwork
2. Quotations
3. Self-Help
4. Ron Kaufman
5. Title

Cover and page layout by The Bonsey Design Partnership.
Cover illustrations by Ngu Hie Ling.
Set in Times and Arial fonts. Printed in Singapore.

Every effort has been made to credit the original author and make full acknowledgement of the source for each quotation in this text. However, if you know of any instance where the quotation or citation could be more accurate, please send a message to Ron@RonKaufman.com Any corrections will gladly be included in future editions. Thank you.

Below each attributed quotation are **quips, quotes and anecdotes in bold text**. These additional notes are by Ron Kaufman (1956 –), who should be cited as the author in all future works.

Ron Kaufman, Lift Me Up!, Pick Me Up!, UP Your Service!, and a balloon with the word *'UP'* are registered trademarks of Ron Kaufman Pte Ltd.

All rights reserved. No part of this book may be reproduced, stored, archived or transmitted in any form by mechanical or electronic means including information storage and retrieval systems without permission in writing from the publisher, except for the quotation of brief passages in book reviews.

Additional copies of this book are available at discount for promotional events, contests, awards and in-house training programs. For details and fast delivery, contact:

Ron Kaufman Pte Ltd
50 Bayshore Park #31-01
Aquamarine Tower
Singapore 469977

Tel: (+65) 6441-2760
Fax: (+65) 6444-8292
Ron@RonKaufman.com
www.RonKaufman.com

Contents

Teamwork works	4
Building a team	29
Team spirit	77
Leading a team	119

Teamwork works

I challenge you to think of one act of genuine significance in the history of humankind that was performed by one lone human being. No matter what you name, you will find a team of people was involved.

John Maxwell

Teamwork is neither 'good' nor 'desirable'. It is a fact. Wherever people work together or play together they do so as a team. Which team to use for what purpose is a crucial, difficult and risky decision that is even harder to unmake. Managements have yet to learn how to make it.

Peter Drucker

One person can achieve something special, but it takes a team to achieve something lasting.

Life is a team sport. Play for *all* your teams to win.

T ogether
E veryone
A chieves
M ore

Rob Gilbert

We are born for co-operation, as are the feet, the hands, the eyelids, and the upper and lower jaws.

Marcus Aurelius

No one can achieve full potential on their own.

People are *designed* to work together.

Men have never been individually self-sufficient.

Reinhold Niebuhr

Alone we can do so little; together we can do so much.

Helen Keller

The self in self-sufficient is a team.

The easiest way to make people better is simply to put them together.

Individuals play the game, but teams win championships.

Roger Staubach

The world basically and fundamentally is constituted on the basis of harmony. Everything works in cooperation with something else.

Preston Bradley

You can work as an individual, but you'll win with a team.

What you do will always influence others.

Teamwork is the ability to work together toward a common vision. The ability to direct individual accomplishments toward organizational objectives. It is the fuel that allows common people to attain uncommon results.

Tom Watson

Nothing of significance was ever achieved by an individual acting alone. Look below the surface and you will find that all seemingly solo acts are really team efforts.

John Maxwell

Is your life fueled for success?

Every solo on the stage requires a team behind the curtain.

We have always found that people are most productive in small teams with tight budgets, timelines and the freedom to solve their own problems.

John Rollwagen

The truth is that teamwork is at the heart of great achievement.

John Maxwell

Don't just make a team – create a winning team.

The greatest achievements are just a team away.

Success depends on the support of other people; the only hurdle between you and what you want is the support of others.

David Schwartz

To be remarkable, be supportable.

Many hands make light work.

Native American saying

The measure of success is not just how many hands are working, but how well they are working together.

Coming together is a beginning, staying together is progress, and working together is success.

Henry Ford

It is through cooperation, rather than conflict, that your greatest successes will be derived.

Ralph Charell

A team, like a machine, comes alive when it is working.

Disagreeing with others may be unavoidable. Cooperating with others is essential.

One person can have a lot of ideas and innovations. But without the teamwork to follow through, these can't be implemented.

Stan Shih

There is no such thing as a self-made man. You will reach your goals only with the help of others.

George Shinn

A good idea may be born in the mind of one, but matures in the hands of many.

If you think you can do it alone, you'll never know how much you could have done.

There are no problems we cannot solve together, and very few that we solve by ourselves.

Lyndon Johnson

If you want to find solutions, hunt for them in teams.

Talent wins games, but teamwork and intelligence win championships.

Michael Jordan

With a team on your side, what victories can you win?

Finding good players is easy. Getting them to play as a team is another story.

Casey Stengel

Light is the task where many share the toil.

Homer

Getting good people together lays a strong foundation. Getting good people to work together gives you strong results.

Is it better to work harder alone, or work smarter with others?

The achievements of an organization are the results of the combined effort of each individual.

Vincent Lombardi

No problem is insurmountable. With a little courage, teamwork and determination, a person can overcome anything.

Bernard Dodge

Individuals count most when they are combined with others.

One person encounters an obstacle. Many people together overcome an obstacle.

People have been known to achieve more as a result of working with others than against them.

Allan Fromme

People moving in opposite directions hold each other back.

The question isn't whether teams have value. The question is whether we acknowledge that fact and become better team players.

John Maxwell

Teams are a reality. How much are they part of yours?

From space, you see earth and earthlings the way God sees us: as one people, unified, working together.

Bernard Harris

No one person can accomplish much if they don't work with others.

Daniel Levinson

Seeing the world through only one set of eyes is a limited point of view. Share your world with others.

If you want to be in it to win, you've got to be in it together.

Coaches and teammates support me. No one can do things alone.

Pelé

Nobody ever came up with a great idea all by themselves.

Thomas Edison

You can run alone, but you score the goals together.

Great things come from great teams.

The only thing that will redeem mankind is cooperation.

Bertrand Russell

The impossible is. possible when people align with you. When you do things with people, not against them, amazing resources are mobilized within.

Gita Bellin

Can you survive alone? Can you excel alone?

More of yourself reveals itself when you align yourself with others.

Even when you've played the game of your life, it's the feeling of teamwork that you'll remember. You'll forget the plays, the shots and the scores, but you'll never forget your team.

Deborah Palmore

Hard work and togetherness. They go hand in hand. You need the hard work because it's tough to win week in and week out. You need togetherness because you don't always win, and then you've got to hang in there together.

Tony Dungy

Facts become part of the past. Feelings stay with you into the future.

Together, the high times get better. Together, the low times seem lesser.

There can be hope only for a society which acts as one big family, not as many separate ones.

Anwar al-Sadat

Teams work better when they work together.

Alice Vernon

The most important family is the one we are all a part of.

If you are not yet working as a team, you are not yet working.

The nice thing about teamwork is that you always have others on your side.

Margaret Carty

Teamwork is so important. It is virtually impossible for you to reach the heights of your capabilities or make the money that you want without becoming good at it.

Brian Tracy

You can't always have everyone on your side. But you can always have someone on your side.

When your teamwork is strong, your results will be strong.

Remember, we all stumble, every one of us. That's why it's a comfort to go hand in hand.

Emily Kimbrough

Call it a clan, call it a network, call it a tribe, call it a family: Whatever you call it, whoever you are, you need one.

Jane Howard

Having someone holding your hand can make the difference between a small stumble and a serious fall.

Everyone needs a team. Appreciate the one you have.

We are all angels with only one wing. We can fly only by embracing each other.

Luciano De Crescenzo

Spending time with your computer can increase your sense of loneliness. Since computers are here to stay, we need to intentionally engage with others.

Lars Wallentin

Everyone has potential to fly when we connect ourselves with others.

Computer connections count, but they are not the whole equation.

It takes two hands to clap.

Chinese proverb

We would rather have one person working with us than three merely working for us.

Dabney Day

What is hard for one to do, can be simple when done with two.

Are people working for you or with you? Are you working for others or with others? Which would you prefer?

The shortest and best way to make your fortune is to let people see clearly that it is in their interest to promote yours.

Jean de la Bruyère

No group as an entity can create ideas. Only individuals can do this. A group of individuals may, however, stimulate one another in the creation of ideas.

Estill Green

When a team wins, there's enough credit and benefit for everyone.

Great ideas can be produced alone, but rarely when people are alone.

We don't accomplish anything in this world alone. Whatever happens is the result of the whole tapestry of one's life, and all the weavings of individual threads from one to another that creates something.

Sandra Day O'Connor

I am pleased to see that we are different. May we together become greater than the sum of both of us.

Vulcan greeting

See beyond who you are to see how much more you are a part of.

Add two that are the same and create something bigger. Add two that are different and create something better.

Building a team

Trust men and they will be true to you: treat them greatly and they will show themselves great.

Ralph Waldo Emerson

When building a team, I always search first for people who love to win. If I can't find any of those, I look for people who hate to lose.

H. Ross Perot

Those who encourage greatness to shine never need to demand it.

You don't have to be coming from the same direction to be aiming for the same place.

Appreciate everything your associates do for the business. Nothing else can quite substitute for a few well-chosen, well-timed and sincere words of praise. They're absolutely free and worth a fortune.

Sam Walton

Others notice how much you notice them.

The leaders who work most effectively have trained themselves not to think 'I'. They think 'we'; they think 'team'. They understand their job is to make the team function. They accept responsibility and don't sidestep it. But 'we' get the credit. This is what creates trust, what enables you to get the task done.

Peter Drucker

Teamwork is more than a smart strategy – it's an elegant understanding.

We try to create conditions where people can come together in a spirit of teamwork, and exercise to their heart's desire their technological capacity.

Akio Morita

To create optimum results, provide optimum conditions.

All winning teams are goal-oriented. Teams like these win consistently because everyone connected with them concentrates on specific objectives. They go about their business with blinders on; nothing will distract them from achieving their aim.

Lou Holtz

Tell a winning team where to go and they will find a way to get there.

When dealing with people, remember you are not dealing with creatures of logic but creatures of emotion.

Dale Carnegie

Treat people as if they were what they ought to be, and you help them to become what they are capable of becoming.

Johann Wolfgang von Goethe

For good results, make business decisions. For the best results, make people decisions.

Treat people as if they have no limits and they will prove to you they don't.

A pat on the back is only a few vertebrae removed from a kick in the pants, but is miles ahead in results.

Ella Wilcox

When your team is winning, be ready to be tough, because winning can make you soft. On the other hand, when your team is losing, stick by them. Keep believing.

Bo Schembechler

Punish for only the most essential reasons. Praise for all the rest.

Whether winning or losing, keep believing.

I wish I had some way to make a bridge from man to man. Man is all we've got.

Kross Daman

Essential to teamwork is trust.

Robert Waterman

A team is the bridge that connects us.

For a team to achieve great results, it must achieve great trust.

The way a team plays as a whole determines its success. You may have the greatest bunch of individual stars in the world, but if they don't play together, the club won't be worth a dime.

George (Babe) Ruth

Teamwork is a make or break situation. Either you help make it or the lack of it will break you.

Kris Hiatt

Each part may be great, but if they don't work together, nothing is accomplished.

Will teamwork make you, or will the lack of teamwork break you?

Too many captains will steer the ship up a mountain.

Chinese proverb

One team, one captain.

There's nothing greater in the world than when somebody on the team does something good, and everybody gathers around to pat him on the back.

Billy Martin

When one person's win is everyone's win, you've got a team that wins.

You don't get harmony
when everybody sings
the same note.

Doug Floyd

**A great team sees
diversity as opportunity,
no argument.**

Man's mind is not a
container to be filled,
but rather a fire to be
kindled.

Dorothea Brande

**Are you smothering the
fire or stoking the fire?**

Strength lies in differences, not in similarities.

Stephen Covey

Honest disagreement is often a good sign of progress.

Mohandas Gandhi

Differences in thinking make a difference.

A good team learns to agree. A great team learns to disagree.

I never criticize a player until they are first convinced of my unconditional confidence in their abilities.

John Robinson

I always prefer to believe the best of everybody – it saves so much trouble.

Rudyard Kipling

Confidence can't be built in a second, but it can be crushed in a second.

Believing people are less than they are is the surest way to make it so.

Once you get people laughing, they're listening and you can tell them almost anything.

Herbert Gardner

If you wish to know the mind of a man, listen to his words.

Chinese proverb

Why break down a barrier with force when you can take it down with pleasure?

Listen to understand what people say and to appreciate who they are.

Every person I work with knows something better than me. My job is to listen long enough to find it and use it.

Jack Nicholas

Listening well is a more powerful means of communication and influence than talking well.

John Marshall

To find out what you know, talk. To learn something new, listen.

You can't make other people listen, but you can make sure you do.

If you think that praise is due, now's the time to show it, because a man can't read his tombstone when he's dead.

Anonymous

If you can laugh together, you can work together.

Robert Orben

Praise now – while you still can.

Happiness is a product of success and a reason for success.

If you put good people in bad systems you get bad results. You have to water the flowers you want to grow.

Stephen Covey

A successful team is a group of many hands with one mind.

Bill Bethel

Gardens need sunshine, nourishment and care. People do, too.

Many minds on a single purpose produce a good result.

You get the best out of others when you give the best of yourself.

Harry Firestone

As you give, so you shall receive.

Every team requires unity. A team has to move as one unit, one force, with each person understanding and assisting the roles of his teammates. If your team doesn't do this, whatever the reason, it goes down in defeat. You win or lose as a team.

Jack Kemp

A team united will not fall.

I won't accept anything less than the best a player's capable of doing. He also has the right to expect the best I can do for him and the team.

Lou Holtz

The best executive is the one who has sense enough to pick good men to do what he wants done, and self-restraint enough to keep from meddling with them while they do it.

Theodore Roosevelt

Why set any standard lower than the best?

Picking the best people gives a good start. Letting them do their best gives a good finish.

Enthusiasm triggers other people's emotions so they instinctively help and support you.

Paul Meyer

Teams do not go physically flat, they go mentally stale.

Vince Lombardi

An inspired team doesn't need to be told.

It's not how much you ask people to do, but how hard you make them think.

You can hire people's hands to work for you, but you must win their hearts for them work with you.

David Schwartz

Are you working with your hands or with all your heart?

The most common cause of team failure is the inability of team members to get along – when there's no trust.

Carol Scearce

If you don't have trust, you don't have a team.

Real teams don't emerge unless individuals on them take risks involving conflict, trust, interdependence and hard work.

Dean Katzenbach

Is there enough room on your team to take a risk?

Conflict is inevitable in a team. To achieve synergistic solutions, a variety of ideas and approaches are needed. And these are the ingredients for conflict.

Susan Gerke

In a synergistic team, conflict is not a problem.

A word of encouragement during a failure is worth more than an hour of praise after success.

Warren Buffett

In order to have a winner, the team must have a feeling of unity; every player must put the team first – ahead of personal glory.

Paul Bryant

When you feel like praising least, it probably matters most.

The team that works together, wins together.

Find that special person who is the heart of the team: they can bring out the best in everybody else.

Mike Krzyzewski

A few honest men are better than numbers.

Oliver Cromwell

The difference between a losing and a winning team can be one special person.

What matters most? How many are on the team or who is on the team?

There are only two options regarding commitment; you're either in or you're out. There's no such thing as life in-between.

Pat Riley

Synergy is the highest activity of life; it creates new untapped alternatives; it values and exploits the mental, emotional and psychological differences between people.

Stephen Covey

If you're not all in, you may as well be out.

Look beyond what is individually possible to discover what is collectively possible.

The key elements in the art of working together are how to deal with change, how to deal with conflict and how to reach your potential. The needs of the team are best met when you meet the needs of individual persons.

Max DePree

Rewards should go to teams as a whole.

Tom Peters

If you want a team to succeed, give each member what they need to succeed.

When everyone wins, everyone feels like a winner.

Many ideas grow better when transplanted into another mind than in the one where they sprung up.

Oliver Wendell Holmes

A team with a star player is a good team, but a team without one can be a great team.

Mario Andretti

A great idea is good. But why not make it better?

The brightest sky is filled with many shining stars.

Teamwork is the quintessential contradiction of a society grounded in individual achievement.

Marvin Weisbord

Synergy is the bonus achieved when things work together harmoniously.

Mark Twain

The more your team challenges the present, the more it can change the future.

A team with synergy requires less and produces more.

A successful team beats with one heart.

Anonymous

How steady is the pulse of your team?

The way to get things done is not to mind who gets the credit for doing them.

Benjamin Jowett

Even better? Make sure others share the credit.

The best way to destroy an enemy is to make him a friend.

Abraham Lincoln

If two men on a job agree all the time, then one is useless. If they disagree all the time, then both are useless.

Darryl Zanuck

If you defeat an enemy, you win once. When you make a friend, you win twice.

Valuable team members are not always in agreement – or disagreement.

Those who are lifting the world upward and onward are those who encourage more than criticize.

Elizabeth Harrison

Correction does much, but encouragement does more.

Johann Wolfgang von Goethe

It's easy to criticize. It's better to encourage.

Ask for more and it might happen. Encourage more and it will happen.

Most of us, swimming against the tides of trouble the world knows nothing about, need only a bit of praise or encouragement and we will make the goal.

Jerome Fleishman

To handle yourself, use your head; to handle others, use your heart.

Donald Laird

A few kind words can produce strong results.

You cannot understand another person only with your mind.

Help thy brother's boat across, and lo! – thine own has reached the shore.

Hindu proverb

If you would lift me up you must be on higher ground.

Ralph Waldo Emerson

Do you ask how others can help you? Or how you can help others?

Are you seeking to receive or to achieve?

Laughter is the shortest distance between two people.

Victor Borge

Never speak of yourself to others; make them talk about themselves instead; therein lies the whole art of pleasing. Everybody knows it, and everyone forgets it.

Jules de Goncourt

One small laugh is more powerful than hours of small talk.

Get yourself out of the spotlight.

I do not speak of what I cannot praise.

Johann Wolfgang von Goethe

It is more difficult to praise rightly than to blame.

Thomas Fuller

If it's not good to hear, it may not be good to say.

Do you choose the best option or the easy option?

Good words are worth much, and cost little.

George Herbert

People don't care about you until they realize how much you care about them.

Dennis Kimbro

It costs the same to say a good word as it does to say a harsh word. But the good word creates more value.

The one who cares most will gain most.

You can't always wait for the guys at the top. Every manager at every level in the organization has an opportunity, big or small, to do something. Every manager's got some sphere of autonomy. Don't pass the buck up the line.

Bob Anderson

It is only as we develop others that we succeed.

Harvey Firestone

Don't let 'not being high enough' be a reason for not reaching higher.

Success comes when you reach beyond yourself.

Individual glory is insignificant when compared to achieving victory as a team.

Dot Richardson

Every great institution is the lengthened shadow of a single man. His character determines the character of the organization.

Ralph Waldo Emerson

If you hoard all the credit, you take away all the joy.

When you create a team, you create more of what you are.

The most serious mistakes are not being made as a result of wrong answers. The truly dangerous thing is asking the wrong question.

Peter Drucker

The best job goes to the person who can get it done without passing the buck or coming back with excuses.

Napoleon Hill

There is no right answer to a wrong question.

Good people do what they can. Great people do what they say they can.

You put together the best team you can with the players you've got, and replace those who aren't good enough.

Robert Crandall

Winning teams are carefully created.

A well-run restaurant is like a winning baseball team. It makes the most of every crew member's talent, and takes advantage of every split-second opportunity to speed up service.

David Ogilvy

To make the best of every opportunity requires the best of every person.

A particular shot or way of moving the ball can be a player's personal signature, but efficiency of performance is what wins the game for the team.

Pat Riley

Amazing things happen when you're nice to the people other people overlook.

Terrie Williams

Do you stand out from the team or stand with the team?

Be nice to those who expect it and you're normal. Be nice to those who don't expect it and you're special.

Everybody in the world wants the same things: to be needed, a job that she or he can do well, to love somebody.

Maya Angelou

It doesn't hurt to help.

Brighten Kaufman

Understanding human nature means understanding each other.

There is no reason good enough for not doing something to help others.

Interdependence is a higher value than independence, but effective inter-dependence can only be built on a foundation of true independence.

Stephen Covey

A silence in the middle of a conversation brings us back to essentials; it reveals how dearly we must pay for the invention of speech.

E.M. Cioran

Before others can depend on you, be sure you can depend on yourself.

Words are powerful. Silence more powerful still.

When you get right to it, and when all is said and done, it is how you connect with people on a personal level that will ensure your success.

Terrie Williams

How successful are your connections?

A group becomes a team when members are sure enough of themselves and their contributions to praise and rely on the skill of others.

Warren Demantis

Those without confidence rely on those who have it.

No man is superior to the game.

Bartlett Giamatti

No manager is an island.

William Oncken, Jr.

Accept the limitations of individual performance. Embrace the greater power of a team.

A good manager builds bridges.

Win together, lose together, play together, stay together.

Debra Mancuso

Everything worth doing, is worth getting done together.

Why should I clutter my mind with general information when I have men around me who can supply any knowledge I need?

Henry Ford

Show others what you know and you seem smart. Find out what they know and you are smarter.

Delegating work works, provided the one delegating works, too.

Robert Half

One man can be a crucial ingredient on a team, but one man cannot make a team.

Kareem Abdul-Jabbar

Setting good goals sets a good example.

To make your success, make your team.

Appreciative words are the most powerful force for good on earth.

George Crane

When you say what good you've seen, you create more good to see.

Teamwork requires people who are willing to help – and people who are willing to be helped.

Ron Kaufman

Can you offer help? Can you accept it?

Share similarities,
celebrate differences.

M. Scott Peck

Out beyond our ideas of
right-doing and wrong-
doing, there is a field.
I'll meet you there.

Rumi

Find how you are the same and you find agreement. Find how you are different and you find fulfillment.

Beyond all judging is our real connection to each other.

Team spirit

Individual commitment to a group effort is what makes a team work, a company work, a society work, a civilization work.

Chauncey Bell

There can only be one state of mind as your team approaches any profound test; total concentration, a spirit of togetherness and strength.

Pat Riley

To achieve something greater, commit to something greater.

When you approach it right, you get it right.

If you are working on the front line, give extra appreciation to those behind the scenes. If you work in the back, remember the power you have to set the mood and morale of those who work out front.

Ron Kaufman

Always try to do something for the other person and you will be agreeably surprised how things come your way – how many pleasing things are done for you.

Claude Bristol

The people in front need a team in the back, and vice versa.

You can't make people do more for you. But you can do more for them.

No member of a crew is praised for the rugged individuality of his rowing.

Ralph Waldo Emerson

If you want to be valued on a team, work with the team.

A player who makes a team great is better than a great player.

John Wooden

Are you trying to be great or to make your team great?

Many engines create power. Many drivers create chaos.

John D. Rockefeller, Jr.

Let one driver to guide your collective power.

It's easy to figure out who isn't a team player. They constantly remind the coach just how good they are.

Brian Jett

Speak less about your part and more about what you're part of.

It is amazing what can be accomplished when everybody shares the credit.

Robert Yates

If a team is to reach its potential, each player must be willing to subordinate his personal goals to the good of the team.

Bud Wilkinson

On a winning team, each win is everyone's win.

Let your team reign supreme.

Place the team above yourself always.

John Wooden

Note how good you feel after you encourage someone else. No other evidence is needed to suggest you never miss an opportunity to encourage.

George Adams

To achieve higher performance, aim for a higher purpose.

When you make another person feel good, you feel good.

It is not the failure of others to appreciate your abilities that should trouble you, but rather your failure to appreciate theirs.

Confucius

If you help others, you will be helped, perhaps tomorrow, perhaps in one hundred years, but you will be helped. Nature must pay off the debt. It is a mathematical law and all life is mathematics.

Gurdjieff

If you want to get more from others, find more in others.

When you help, you make a deposit. Life pays good interest.

People may not remember exactly what you did or said, but they will always remember how you made them feel.

Ruth Kaufman

A connection creates an impression.

When I am getting ready to reason with a person, I spend one-third of my time thinking about myself and what I am going to say and two-thirds about him and what he is going to say.

Abraham Lincoln

What is more valuable? Knowing what you think or finding out what the other person thinks?

Be a good listener. Your ears will never get you in trouble.

Frank Tyger

The six most important words: I admit I made a mistake. The five most important words: You did a good job. The four most important words: What is your opinion? The three most important words: If you please. The two most important words: Thank you. The one least important word: I.

Anonymous

Have you ever met a person who listened too much? How did you know? Who was doing all the talking?

It's important to know what's important – and what's not.

Most teams aren't teams at all but merely collections of individual relationships with the boss. Individuals vying for power, prestige and position actually weakens a team.

Douglas Mcgregor

Everyone has a vast capacity for being more understanding, respectful, warm, genuine, open and direct in human relationships.

George Gazda

In a strong team, no one vies for attention because everyone knows they are valued.

Inspire yourself to live at your highest level.

I feel the greatest reward is the opportunity to do more.

Jonas Salk

The weak can never forgive. Forgiveness is the attribute of the strong.

Mohandas Gandhi

You can't always get more, but you can always choose to give more.

To test your strength, forgive someone now. To build your strength, forgive someone forever.

When you care, you win. Too many people are so involved in getting the job done or in doing what they consider their own work, they forget to use common sense – which is treating people as you would like to be treated.

Donna Edton

Team spirit is what gives so many companies an edge over their competitors.

George Clements

People are not minor details. They don't deserve minor attention.

Let the spirit of team become the spirit of many.

The most important measure of how good a game I played was how much better I'd made my teammates play.

Bill Russell

Good players can sometimes play great. But great players can make others play great.

If you wish to make a man your enemy, tell him simply, 'You are wrong.' This method works every time.

Henry Link

So simple, so devastating.

We should be lenient in our judgment, because often the mistakes of others would have been ours had we had the opportunity to make them.

Benjamin Alsaker

The words you speak today should be soft and tender, for tomorrow you may have to eat them.

Anonymous

Learn from the mistakes of others as if they were your own.

Even what is right today may be wrong by the dawning of tomorrow.

Getting people to like you is merely the other side of liking them.

Norman Vincent Peale

Constant kindness can accomplish much. As the sun makes ice melt, kindness causes misunderstanding, mistrust and hostility to evaporate.

Albert Schweitzer

Start with the other side to get people on your side.

One kind act is simple. Many kind acts are powerful.

The important thing to recognize is that it takes a team, and the team ought to get credit for the wins and the losses. Successes have many fathers, failures have one.

Philip Caldwell

Simply stated, teamwork is less me and more we.

Anonymous

Share credit in the wins. Share learning in the losses.

Think only of yourself and you miss what you are a part of.

You don't do things right once in a while. You do them right all the time.

Vince Lombardi

You will find men who want to be carried on the shoulders of others, who think that the world owes them a living. They don't seem to see that we must all lift and pull together.

Henry Ford

Success is not achieved by your greatest act, but by the sum of all your acts.

When everyone pulls together, everyone is uplifted.

Acceptance of others, their looks, behaviors and beliefs, brings you an inner peace and tranquillity instead of anger and resentment.

Byron Katie

Who angers you, conquers you.

Aristotle

Acceptance is a powerful choice.

You don't always have the power to control, but you always have the power to respond.

You may be deceived if you trust too much, but you will live in torment if you don't trust enough.

Frank Crane

Do not condemn the judgment of another because it differs from your own. You may both be wrong.

Dandemis

Are you afraid of trusting too much or guilty of trusting too little?

If you want to find the truth, be open to all truths.

He who wishes to secure the good of others has already secured his own.

Confucius

Only strength can cooperate. Weakness can only beg.

Dwight D. Eisenhower

When you act to help others you have already helped yourself.

The test isn't whether you're strong enough to work alone, but whether you're strong enough to work together.

Forgiveness is the sweetest revenge.

Isaac Friedmann

We achieve inner health only through forgiveness – the forgiveness not only of others but also of ourselves.

Joshua Leibman

When forgiveness is given, freedom is earned.

Forgiveness prevents past mistakes from creeping into tomorrow.

Forgiveness is not for their benefit, but for our own.

Ron Kaufman

A winner rebukes and forgives; a loser is too timid to rebuke and too petty to forgive.

Sidney Harris

Forgive – not because someone asks you to, but because you ask it of yourself.

A strong person can hold on. A stronger person can let go.

Whenever you are confronted with an opponent, conquer him with love.

Mohandas Gandhi

If an opponent hates, can adding more hate ever help?

The control center of your life is your attitude.

Tiffany Merchant

If you want to do something better, change your actions. If you want to do everything better, change your attitude.

Sometimes your joy is the source of your smile, but sometimes your smile can be the source of your joy.

Thich Nhat Hanh

Smile in joy. Smile to create joy.

Deal with the faults of others as gently as with your own.

Chinese proverb

The faults of others are always near your own. Tread carefully.

We have two ears and one mouth so that we can listen twice as much as we speak.

Epictetus

So when you are listening to somebody, completely and attentively, then you are listening not only to the words, but also to the feeling of what is being conveyed – to the whole of it, not part of it.

Jiddu Krishnamurti

Do you listen as well as you could? Do you listen as much as you should?

When you listen fully, you hear more than words.

A blow with a word strikes deeper than a blow with a sword.

Robert Burton

Sharp words leave deep impressions.

The same fence that shuts others out shuts you in.

William Taylor

Keep the gates of cooperation wide open.

If you cannot work with love but only with distaste it is better that you should leave your work.

Kahlil Gibran

Love it or leave it.

Efficiency is doing better what is already being done.

Peter Drucker

Do something better and you are sure to improve.

You don't get the breaks unless you play with the team instead of against it.

Lou Gehrig

The moment we break faith with one another, the sea engulfs us and the light goes out.

James Baldwin

If you're not playing together, you're not playing.

Lack of trust is the reason for failing, not the result of failing.

The ratio of *We's* to *I's* is the best indicator of development in a team.

Lewis Ergen

What side of the balance are you on?

A smile is a curve that can set things straight.

Leo Buscalia

A smile moves things in the right direction.

Nothing is ever lost by courtesy. It is the cheapest of pleasures; costs nothing and conveys much. It pleases the one who gives and the one who receives, and thus, like mercy, it is twice blessed.

Erastus Wiman

Can a person be too pleasant or polite? How often does that happen?

Kindness is a language which the deaf can hear and the blind can read.

Mark Twain

Never lose an opportunity to use that special language.

No one is useless in this world who lightens the burden of another.

Charles Dickens

Everybody on a championship team doesn't get publicity, but everyone can say he's a champion.

Earvin (Magic) Johnson

You can't always remove another person's burden, but you can often help them carry it.

You don't have to be in the spotlight to be the reason the spotlight is shining.

I think any player will tell you that individual accomplishment helps your ego. But if you don't win, it makes for a very, very long season. It counts more that the team has played well and won.

David Robinson

The force is within you. Force yourself.

Harrison Ford

A good team competes against other teams. A great teams never competes with itself.

It's only potential until you make it happen.

You cannot shake hands with a clenched fist.

Indira Gandhi

Don't be afraid to give your best to what are seemingly small jobs. Every time you conquer one it makes you that much stronger. If you do little jobs well, the big ones tend to take care of themselves.

Dale Carnegie

Open your mind and you'll open some doors. Open your heart and the doors will open to you.

Small things done with great focus lead to greatness.

People take different roads seeking fulfillment and happiness. Just because they are not on your road does not mean they are lost.

Jackson Browne

When anger rises, think of the consequences.

Confucius

If everyone looks for the same thing, no one discovers anything new.

Feel anger and it will pass. Act with anger and it will last.

Animals don't hate, and we're supposed to be better than them.

Elvis Presley

The only way to get the best of an argument is to avoid it.

Dale Carnegie

Hate makes you less than you are capable of being.

Duck the arguments flying around you.

Politeness is the art of choosing among one's real thoughts.

Adlai Stevenson

Etiquette means behaving yourself a little better than is absolutely essential.

Will Cuppy

Say the first thing on your mind and you speak quickly. Say the best thing on your mind and you speak well.

That little extra step will take you far.

To err is human, to forgive divine.

Alexander Pope

He who has not forgiven an enemy has not yet tasted one of the most sublime enjoyments of life.

Johann Lauter

Error reveals that you are human. Forgiveness confirms it.

Forgiveness matters when it challenges you the most.

Write kindness in marble. Write injuries in the dust.

Persian proverb

To carry a grudge is like being stung to death by one bee.

William Walton

Remembering good adds to your future. Remembering pain only adds to your pain.

Grudges make persistent the things that should have been forgotten.

We never listen when we are eager to speak.

François de La Rochefoucauld

You wouldn't worry so much about what people thought of you if you knew just how seldom they actually do.

Leonard Orr

Think less about what you want say and more about what is being said.

Think less about what others think and they'll think more of you.

I have often regretted my speech, never my silence.

Abraham Lincoln

Words not said never need to be taken back.

The best time to hold your tongue is the time you feel you must say something or bust.

Josh Billings

There is wisdom in keeping to yourself.

Speak when you are angry and you'll make the best speech you'll ever regret.

Lawrence Peter

A word is not a bird. It cannot be put back in the cage.

Russian proverb

When you are angry, speak to yourself.

You can't take a memory away, but you can avoid putting it there.

4

Leading a team

What creates trust, in the end, is the leader's manifest respect for the followers.

Jim O'Toole

Trust cannot be demanded. It must be earned.

I have no pride. I'll do anything necessary to get people involved. I am a dispenser of enthusiasm.

Benjamin Zander

Will you do what it takes, no matter what it takes?

I've always found that the speed of the boss is the speed of the team.

Lee Iacocca

Leadership creates conditions where people *want* to do what needs to be done.

Sim Kay Wee

The person at the front of the race always sets the pace.

Demanding action is not the same as desiring action. One is the style of a boss, the other is the accomplishment of a leader.

Setting a vision is the domain of leaders.

Monte Moses

Leadership means vision, cheerleading, enthusiasm, love, trust, passion, obsession, consistency, creating heroes, coaching and numerous other things.

Tom Peters

A leader makes appear what is not yet there.

Leadership means doing whatever is needed.

A mission is worthless unless it is put to work.

George Patterson

My most important contribution was my ability to pick strong and intelligent men and then hold the team together by persuasion, by apologies, by financial incentives, by speeches, by chatting with their wives and by using every tool at my command to make that team think I was a decent guy.

Thomas Watson, Jr.

A mission described is a vision. A mission in action is real.

Anything less than whatever it takes is simply not enough.

I don't believe in team motivation. I believe in getting a team prepared so it has the necessary confidence when it steps on a field to play a good game.

Tom Landry

The key to successful leadership today is influence, not authority.

Ken Blanchard

Great preparation and a clear direction need no further motivation.

If you want compliant people, make demands. If you want inspired people, make suggestions.

Great leaders exude self-confidence. They are never petty. They are never buck-passers. They pick themselves up after defeat.

David Ogilvy

Good leaders make people feel they are at the very heart of things, not at the periphery. Everyone feels they make a difference to the success of the organization. When that happens, people feel centered and that gives their work meaning.

Warren Bennis

Confidence in yourself inspires confidence in others.

Leaders make people feel like they are a very important part of something very important.

A good leader is not the person who does everything right, but the person who finds the right things for everyone to do.

Anthony Dadovano

If your actions inspire others to dream more, learn more, do more and become more, you are a leader.

John Quincy Adams

The right people doing the right things get the right results. The wrong people doing the wrong things get no results.

Do you ask people to be what they are, or inspire them to be what they can become?

All resources are not obvious; great leaders find and develop available talent.

Dwight D. Eisenhower

The best kept secret in business today is that people would rather work hard for something they believe in than enjoy a pampered, idle life.

John Gardner

Before visions can come to life, people must come to life.

Give people a challenge to achieve and they will take it.

A smile when giving criticism can make the difference between resentment and reform.

Phillip Steinmetz

Criticism should not be querulous and wasting, but guiding, instructive and inspiring.

Ralph Waldo Emerson

Be honest but be kind.

Criticism takes effort to hear. Make sure the effort has its rewards.

The most dangerous leadership myth is that leaders are born – that there is a genetic factor to leadership. This myth asserts that people simply either have certain charismatic qualities or not. That's nonsense; in fact, the opposite is true. Leaders are made rather than born.

Warren Bennis

I start with the premise that the function of leadership is to produce more leaders, not more followers.

Ralph Nader

A leader is not who you were, but who you can become.

Give people the room they need to grow.

Leadership is a combination of strategy and character. If you must be without one, be without the strategy.

Norman Schwarzkopf

Leadership is lifting a person's vision to higher sights, raising a person's performance to a higher standard, building a personality beyond its normal limitations.

Peter Drucker

Where does character sit in your hierarchy of importance?

The strongest leader is the one who lifts others the highest.

Without leadership, nothing happens.

Michael Hammer

Leaders walk their talk; in true leaders, there is no gap between the theories they espouse and their practice.

Warren Bennis

If nothing is happening, don't ask what is missing, ask who is missing.

Leaders do not create standards, they live the standards.

The first rule of leadership is to save yourself for the big decisions. Don't allow your mind to be cluttered with trivia.

Richard Nixon

The first quality of the commander-in-chief is a cool head to receive a correct impression of things. He should not allow himself to be confused either by good or bad news.

Napoleon Bonaparte

Leaders must keep the big picture in focus.

Change the conditions. Don't let the conditions change you.

I've made my share of mistakes – plenty of them – but my biggest mistake by far was not moving faster to correct a mistake. Pulling an old bandage one hair at a time hurts a lot more than a sudden yank.

Jack Welch

Great leaders are always fanatically committed to their jobs. They do not suffer from the crippling need to be universally loved.

David Ogilvy

Why prolong a painful act? If it needs to be done, do it quickly.

When you are fanatically commited, you'll reach your goals.

How you handle your time is, in my view, the single most important aspect of being a role model and leader.

Andrew Grove

Too many instructions to employees are often fatal. Don't be too specific; such an attitude makes a man into a machine.

Richard Sears

If your employees did what you do, would you be impressed?

Limiting people limits results.

If I've got a fault, it's probably that I manage hands-on too much. You shouldn't get so antsy that your people don't even have the time to find out where the bathroom is.

Lee Iacocca

People know more than you think. Give them a chance to prove it.

I never hesitated to promote someone I didn't like. I looked for those sharp, scratchy, harsh, almost unpleasant people who see and tell you about things as they really are.

Thomas Watson, Jr.

The hardest things to hear are often those that can help you the most.

Thank you for choosing, reading and sharing this book with others. From the 512 magnificent quips and practical tips, this one is my favorite:

> We are all angels with only one wing. We can fly only by embracing each other.
> – Luciano De Crescenzo

Which quote do you most embrace? With whom will you share it, and fly in life together?

Wishing you a joyful flight!

To order more copies of the **Lift Me Up!**® books, visit your local bookstore or www.LiftMeUpBooks.com